Simple Tips to

Writing Your Non-Fiction Book

In 30 Days or Less

RALI MACAULAY

Presented To:

_____

From:

_____

Date:_____

RALI MACAULAY

CONTENTS

Introduction

Have you had a great idea for years, or even just recently, that you desire to put in a book? Perhaps you always wanted to write a book, but just never seem to be able to get started? You may even have started at one time or the other, but got stuck, and just never finished writing the book, not to mention getting it published.

Writing a book from start to finish can sometimes look like a daunting task, but it needn't be! I struggled for several years to get my first book idea from mere thoughts and wishes into an actual book, only to discover that I did not need to have used that many years to write a book. In fact my next book after that was completed and ready for publishing in about a month! Ever since, I have been able to finish writing my books way faster than when I first started.

However, not knowing how to get from the ideas you have to a completed book can make writing your book look like an impossible task. When you know what to do, you will find it so much easier that you can't wait to write your book, and the next.

As you will find as you read this book, the only limiting factor for the most part is you, the Writer. A lot depends on what time and effort you are willing to give to your dream of completing your book.

This book will guide you on how to turn those ideas in your head, into a book. Many have done it. You too can.

My desire is to show you simple tips you can apply to start and complete writing your book. These are the same tips I applied, and still use in writing my books. When I started to apply these tips, I began to see rapid productivity in my book-writing endeavors; and have been able to write my books in a much shorter period of time than when I first started out.

I have since then acquired more skills and experience, of course, because the more you do a thing, the better you'll be at it. These are what I will be sharing with you on this journey of going from your ideas to a book.

My hope is that the experiences and principles I have gathered, and applied, as an Author, being shared in this book, will help anyone who have struggled to complete writing a book, or has never even tried writing, but wants to.

Chapter 1

Why Write a Book?

Many people may have great ideas for books, but not everyone writes a book! Even the exceptionally talented may never get to finish or publish their book, regardless of how much they desire to. Why? Because there is a huge difference between desiring to, knowing how to, and actually writing.

But why should you write a book?

We all have unique life experiences, talents, skills, stories, businesses, accomplishments…whatever it is, we do have something that can be beneficial to others. Besides, you never know what ideas of yours can positively impact other people's lives, until you share it. Writing a book comes with so many benefits, some of which are mentioned below:

- **You touch and add value to lives:** You impact the lives of other people, many of whom you will never meet in person. When you share valuable information, your books will not only touch lives, but will also help your readers achieve their own dreams too.

- **You leave a legacy:** Many good books are still here long after their Authors are gone. Such books are still positively influencing lives many years after. That is how powerful a book is. When you share your knowledge and expertise with the world too, chances are your books will be a legacy many years down the road.

- **Satisfaction and sense of accomplishment:** When you eventually complete and publish your book, it fills you with a deep sense of satisfaction. You feel accomplished and motivated to do other seemingly difficult tasks.

- **Opens you up to opportunities:** As a published Author, you stand a greater chance for opportunities both in your current business, as well as new ones. For example, your writing can open you up for speaking engagements, coaching/training opportunities; as well as opportunities to develop and sell new products.

- **Exposure:** In addition to the above, you become known and recognized as an expert in your field when you publish a book.

- **Income Stream:** Publishing and selling your books means you begin to earn some form of income, either through royalties or direct sales. You can also create leads that help you sell other products from your book.

- **Passive Income:** Once your book is written and published, you don't have to re-write the same book over and over to continue to make income from it. You write it once, and continue on to the next thing you desire to do. While you are busy with other areas of your life, your book continues to make you some income.

- **You become an inspiration for others:** Whether you know it or not, someone somewhere will be inspired seeing you become an author. When you publish your book, someone else, that you may never know or meet, will be motivated to complete their book as well. There will be others you know personally, who have desires to be authors that will have renewed hope that it is possible for them too just because they have seen you do it.

How long will it take?

Some have written books in a month, some less. Yet others have taken years. How soon you complete writing your book will largely depend on how much time and efforts you are willing to put into it; as well as your commitment to actually writing the book. It will also partly depend on the length of each book. But even lengthy books don't have to take forever if you follow the tips offered in this book.

There have been several authors that have written 50,000 words in a month! Even though you may not aim for that many words, my point is you can complete writing your book within that time frame; and then move on to the publishing phase. As a matter of fact, for a non-fiction book, you don't need that many words to make a book.

Chapter 2

Qualities of a Writer

Do you have what it takes?

Several people desire to write, but are too afraid to even get started. Why? Because they think they will fail even before they begin writing. It may be that they know no one personally who has ever published, so they think it's only for certain people with special talents.

Don't get me wrong, you do need some skills, and natural talents are great too; but even with those, you will still need to learn one or two things here and there, on your journey to becoming an Author. There will always be something new to learn.

But don't be intimidated, and refuse to be frightened out of your desire to write. If you have written emails before, or even voiced your opinion on social media platforms, and enjoy doing so, then you can write!

What you need is knowing how to collate and develop your opinion, ideas, and thoughts into a continuous flow that makes sense to a reader. I will be showing you how to do this later on in this book.

Having a sincere desire to write, and having the love to write, to an extent, is also a big plus. You must be passionate about sharing knowledge, and helping others learn too.

As a Writer, you must be:

- Disciplined enough to stick to your schedules and deadlines

(more on this later)

- Tenacious, able to continue what you started and not giving up

- Willing and able to learn new things; and to continue learning

- Strong enough to overcome procrastinations

- Focused

- Hardworking

- Professional

In addition, don't be distracted by some of the excuses and fears commonly expressed by prospective Authors. Some of which are:

- No one will like my book: You don't know that until you actually write one. Focus your energy on writing your book first, and don't worry about that. Give it your best. It is actually natural to feel like that, especially with your first book, so don't let that thought put you off.

- No one will buy it: If you have done your initial topic research well, as explained in this book, you probably will have an audience willing to pay for your knowledge.

- I don't have a special talent for writing: Majority of writers that became bestsellers didn't have any "special talents" for writing, but were willing to learn and give it their all.

- I'm not an English major: You don't need to be one.

- I don't have the time to write: You

probably never will, but you can make the time as I'll explain later.

- I'm not educated enough: Many college drop-outs have been known to write books that changed lives, and became bestsellers.

Thoughts like the ones above have kept many with great potentials from writing or ever getting published. If you have any of such fears, I hope that changes by the end of this book.

Remember that as long as you never get started, you will never know how much you can do, or how far you can go. You will never know what opportunities are out there for you as an Author if you never take that first step.

Believe in yourself, that you can write a book! Yes, you! Regardless of your time constraint, financial status, or lack of academic excellence in the past, you still can write a book!

Let your focus be on your ability to help someone somewhere through your book. Never disregard that possibility. Believe in yourself, and in your book.

Constantly tell yourself that you are writing an excellent and helpful book. I'm not talking of bragging to others, but rather making positive affirmations to yourself.

Get past your fears and the myths you have heard about writing and believe in your capabilities.

Chapter 3

Getting Started

The water does not start flowing until the facet is turned on – Louis L'Amour

My first book, "Scripture Works!" took me over 10 years to finish! Even though I was greatly passionate about the topic, and it was one that was almost natural to me, yet that was not enough to get the book completed and published.

However, when I finally changed the methods that were not working, it took me just few months to go from a scattered disorganized outline to a published book that hit the bestseller list in at least 3 categories few hours after it launched; and remained on the bestseller list several months after.

So what changed?

One of the first things that I needed to do was make a commitment to myself to get it done regardless of the distractions and limitations. As a result of this, I had to set realistic goals for myself, and decide what needed to be sacrificed for this goal of completing my book.

I also had to figure out how to get past those times when I just didn't feel like writing, and stick to my writing schedules.

No matter how excited you are as you start your book, many writers will agree that sometimes you hit a brick wall, or so it seems. This is what some call "writer's block". It is that state where you just can't think of anything to write that makes good sense; or you simply just lack the motivation to write anything.

You catch yourself giving excuses on why you can't write "right now", but rather doing something else or even nothing at all.

Well, it happens to the best of us, but what makes a victor, is the person that pushes past those times and feelings to get done what they really should be doing.

Below are some tips to get you started and motivated to complete your book.

Tips to Help You Succeed as You Write Your Book:

Discipline and Commitment

It takes discipline and commitment to find ways, and time, to write. Very few, if any, succeed without discipline and commitment. As fun as it sounds to be an Author, it demands diligence and discipline.

It takes discipline to make yourself write when you don't feel like it; when something more fun is calling for your attention. It also takes commitment to return to your book writing after taking scheduled breaks.

Self Development

Learn, learn and learn again. Invest in yourself. Someone rightly said when you stop learning, you "die". No matter your level of intelligence and expertise, there will always be something new to learn.

Make yourself available for new ideas and inspirations, and never be ashamed of learning something new, or asking questions. In every way you can, see to it that you improve your writing skills.

Consistency

A never giving up attitude is crucial to your success as an Author.

There will be many times, and logical reasons too, why you just feel like calling it quits with your dream of becoming an Author, but you must purpose in your heart to not give up until you see your finished book in your hands.

If you have decided to write at a particular time, be consistent and keep to that time. If there is a routine you have chosen to help you get to your goal, don't give up; keep at it consistently, except if you realize it is absolutely not going to work, or is unrealistic.

Set a Deadline:

Nothing keeps you motivated like a deadline. Think of it; when someone, or a company gives you a deadline, and it's linked to a promotion you desperately need, for example, what do you do? You create the time to work on it. You give it your best shot, and see to it that you meet that deadline, which you otherwise may have procrastinated on! That is the power of a deadline.

Personally when I don't set deadlines for my projects, things tend to drag endlessly. But when I set specific deadlines, it helps me be disciplined to map out my strategies and commit to my goal. That is when I begin to see things done in record time!

Try this as well. Set a rough deadline for yourself at first. Make it as realistic as possible. Later on in this book, I have given a suggested plan based on a 30 day deadline/schedule. If you feel you need more time for your first book, by all means adjust as you feel appropriate. But note that you can write your book in 30 days, and many have written a book in less time than that.

After you set a deadline, further break your plan into smaller tasks and time frames.

- Set due dates for things like outline completion, cover completion, editing, formatting and the likes
- Set a book launch date. What date do you want your book launched? Be specific.

Identify Barriers and Distractions:

What has been making writing your book difficult? Do you feel you don't have the time? Is it that you have "too much on your plate" already?

A good starting point is to identify what takes up your time, making it impossible for you to write your book. Take out a piece of paper, or a note app on your phone, and list what your challenges are. Make them short and straight to the point.

The goal here is to determine how to

eliminate, or at least drastically reduce these barriers/distractions.

Set Your Priorities:

Now that you have identified your challenges to writing your book, take a critical look at your list. How important to your life goals are these?

Mark those activities you absolutely can't do without. Note which ones are not so important. Compare these to your desire of being an Author. Can you at least put some of these on hold while you go after the goal of finishing your book?

Schedule Time for Writing:

A common excuse is lack of time. Many believe they would complete their books if only they had the time. You never will have the time; you have to make the time.

There will always be something craving for your time and attention, so don't keep delaying your writing until you have some time. No matter how busy your schedule, when you give it careful attention, you can always find ways to make time to write.

From our exercise of setting your priorities, you must have identified the different areas and activities you spend your time on. This will help you see where you can carve out time for writing.

Identify the daily activities you can eliminate, at least for a short while. It could be time spent on social media, watching your favorite shows on TV, or just lounging on your sofa, doing nothing. These are times you can divert to writing your book.

From your daily schedule; what time in the day (or which days of the week) can you commit to your writing? Make a note of these.

Making time to write could also mean waking up earlier than usual to write for an hour or so every day. If you are a stay-at-home parent, it could be your kid's nap time, or at night after your kids are all in bed.

Once you have identified what time or days work best for you, schedule your daily or weekly writing times, and make yourself write during those times. Make a routine of it. Having a routine helps boost your productivity, as you write your book.

Next, decide how long you will write

each day or week. It could be 30 minutes, one hour, or more. You can also decide ahead of time how many words you plan to write during your scheduled time. Just make sure it is something doable, considering your other responsibilities.

If possible commit to writing at the very least an hour a day (If you can write more hours daily, the better). If you can't fit one full hour at a stretch into your schedule, break it into two 30 minutes time frames; maybe 30 minutes in the morning, and 30 minutes in the evening.

Whatever you do, write as scheduled. Don't try to make it pretty just yet. Concentrate on getting your ideas out in writing first. You'll edit later.

Know for sure that you'll have many opportunities to drift away to more fun things, especially when the ideas are not flowing as much, but be disciplined enough to stick to the times you have decided on.

Remember, anything of value will cost you something; but it is such a rewarding feeling to know you disciplined yourself enough to earn the success you desired.

Action Tips:

Put down the answer to the questions below somewhere, and keep it before your eyes as often as possible (your writing spot is not a bad idea).

When you sit to write:

- How long do you plan to write for? (How many hours or minutes?)

- How many words are you aiming for?

- How often do you want to write? Daily, every other day, weekends, mornings, evenings?

The more time you can make out to write, the better.

Designate Writing Spot:

It is best if you have a designated, organized place for your writing. This too will help increase your productivity.

Choose a place with minimal distractions. If needed, you may even decide to get out of your comfort zone sometimes, and go do your writing somewhere outside your home (in the library perhaps, or some other conducive place).

Do the "Write" thing!

Without actually doing the writing exercise, all the other steps are mere waste of time. Get started.

As important as planning your book is, don't get stuck planning for ever. Set a time limit for your planning, and move on to writing. You can always add more to your plans, or change it as you want later on; but no matter what, start writing. You will never finish what you don't start, so start - today!

As you start writing your book, what you write may not look or sound too brilliant, but don't give up, keep writing.

You'll be amazed that what you thought was not good may actually be what people are looking to read! Don't be afraid to write. Just do it.

The more you write, the better your

writing will be, and the more the ideas for what to write will start flowing.

Announce it to the "World":

Why should you do this? It makes you even more committed to finishing your book especially when you give a "coming soon" date. I do this for my books.

Creating a buzz about your book before its release date is a smart thing to do. In addition to helping you finish what you started, it will also help boost your sales when the book is finally released.

A great place to make your announcement is social media where you already have a following.

You can also pass the message

across by word of mouth to those around you. However, I'd advise you speak to people you know will cheer you on, as you need all the support you can get right now. If you are not sure of a person, leave them out of the announcement.

You cannot finish what you never started…Start writing

Chapter 4

Choosing a Book Topic

As you start to plan your book, it is important to choose topics that will solve problems. These are the kind of books people will be interested in, and as a result, are the books that sell.

In other words, choose topics people are already interested in. Ask yourself, "Is there a need for this book?" You should write a book that will help and positively impact people's lives; and not just write to say you're an Author.

Tips on Where to Get Inspirations for a Book Topic

What People Are Searching for Online

Forums and search engines are great ways to find topics to write on. Google your proposed topics; are people searching for these information already? What specifically do they need answers for?

Don't be discouraged if others are writing on the same topic already. The beauty of the human learning process is a person can hear the same message they have heard before, but presented in a slightly different way, and they get it this time, even when they didn't get it all along.

So never think you are duplicating another person's effort. Just be original in your approach and adapt your own style. There are people out there that understand the topic better the way you present it.

Amazon is another great place to find if readers want your book. By searching your idea, you should be able to come up with books on ideas similar to yours. If you do, you may have a market for your book.

Of course, it is not impossible to come up with brand new ideas and create a market for it, but just make sure there are enough people in the globe interested in your idea.

Your Passion

What are you passionate about? What is that one thing that you can keep talking about almost endlessly? What are you good at that almost requires no effort from you to do? This may be a good place to start!

Writing about what you love doing is a great way to start your writing career. Because you are passionate about this topic, it will most likely flow naturally to you.

Life Experiences

Life experiences are a great source of ideas for your book. People like to read about the experiences of others, especially if they have similar situations in their lives, and are seeking help or guidance.

So never underestimate the importance of your life stories. You never know, your story may just be what that other person needs to read at a particular time in their life.

In fact readers love when you add your personal stories to your book; when you show you are a real person, with real challenges that you managed to overcome. They want to know how you did it.

Your Expertise and Talents

Are you an expert in any particular field or topic? Well, maybe you don't consider yourself an expert, but are you constantly having answers for people regarding particular issues or topics? Are people often contacting you with questions on certain matters?

Many times we take our talents and expertise for granted and don't recognize them as such. But when you think about it, those things or tasks you find so easy to do may be very difficult for others; and some will gladly pay to learn from your book.

Take a look at your everyday activities, what topics do you easily and freely contribute too? These are topics you may enjoy writing a book on.

Your Blog Posts

If you already have a blog, your blog posts may be a good place to look for ideas, particularly if you have already developed a good following.

Which blog posts attracted the most comments? Which posts were most popular among your site visitors or fans? Which ones attracted the most interaction? These will make good topics for you to write on.

Your Past Articles

This is closely related to the blog post above, however this is not usually a post on your own personal blog. You may have written an article in the past that may or may not be published; this can be a good outline for your next book.

New Discoveries: Teach What You're Learning

One of the best ways to retain new knowledge is teaching it to others. The more you teach others what you just learnt, the better you understand it; and the greater your chances of being recognized as an expert on that topic.

If you are breaking into new discoveries, or gaining new information that excites you, this may be a good topic for you to write on.

Research

It is also possible for you to pick a topic you're not too familiar with, but which perhaps you are inquisitive about.

In such cases you'll be doing researches to collate the necessary information to share in your book. You may even write a book that brings together the ideas of different experts on a single topic. However, when you do this, it is important to not plagiarize, but to give credits to these experts; as well as letting your readers know you are presenting information from these experts.

Interviews

You can also base your book on live interviews you conducted on several individuals. Based on your agreement with the people you interview, you may, or may not include their real names in your book.

Questions People Are Asking

When people are asking a lot of questions on a particular topic either online through search engines, forums, social media, or offline as you relate with people on the job, school, social gathering etc (or if you notice people struggling with particular issues); these could potentially give you something to write about.

Your Past Audio/Video Teachings

If you have prior work you taught in person, on audio or even videos, these can be transcribed into a book. However, make sure you thoroughly edit it so it makes sense to a reader as your audience is now different from the original audience.

Random Thoughts and Ideas

Sometimes, you may have ideas pop up in your head, particularly as you begin to give serious thoughts to writing a book.

Don't discard these. Capture them somewhere; either on paper or whatever you have available. I sometimes use the voice memo app on my phone if I get an idea that I'm not able to type or pen down immediately.

Chapter 5

Your Book Title

One of the things that make a great book is a great title. A common dilemma often faced by authors (both seasoned and new) is what to call their book. For many it is a struggle even long after the book is written.

Your book title is one of the most important parts of your book. It can be the deciding factor for your book sales and even for getting on a bestseller's list.

Your book title is one of the very first things a reader sees and considers before making the decision whether or not to buy or read your book.

This means titles are very important.

As such, what you decide to call your book matters a lot. It can make or mar your book, so choose your book titles carefully and thoughtfully.

Tips on Choosing a Book Title

In deciding on an appropriate title for your book, make a list of several titles that comes to mind based on the topic you are writing on.

List as much as you can - at least 10 titles, the more the better. Browse through these and eliminate those that absolutely don't fit your book topic.

You may also want to share with others for their opinion. If you are getting feedback that is different from what you intends your book to portray, then you should consider reviewing or discarding such titles.

No matter what title you eventually choose for your book, certain parameters must be put into consideration:

- Pick a title that is easy to search on the platform you intend to publish on. Research key words. Which ones come up most? What books are bestsellers in your niche market, and what kind of titles do they have?

- Make your titles as short and simple as possible. Avoid overly long titles. You can always add subtitles, but make your actual titles short and straight to the point.

- What is the message in your book? Your title should give a prospective reader a glimpse of what to expect from the book. It should convey the message/benefits in your book to your readers. What will the reader gain by reading the book?

- Let your title be inviting. You want a title that captivates the reader or audience. It should stand out enough to attract the audience you are targeting; and encourage a reader to, at least, view your book.

Subtitles

Subtitles are equally important in convincing a reader to choose your book out of the several others out there. Here are some tips to help you decide on what subtitle to use for your book:

- Let your subtitle pass across the message of what your book will do for the reader
- Let the subtitle be focused and specific, not confusing
- Your subtitle should not contradict, but rather

compliment, your book title

- Keep it as short as possible
- Make it effective enough to "sell" your book

Chapter 6

Steps to Writing Your Book

As you start your book, it is highly recommended to follow proven steps to take you from the idea conception to the finished product you desire. I will keep these steps as simple and straight forward as possible.

Step 1: Do a brain dump

What ideas are playing around in your mind? Pouring them all out somewhere as an initial step is what is meant by a brain dump.

It is simply a process where you "empty" the ideas in your mind about the book topic on a blank page, paper, a board, or whatever you decide to use. This is same as what some call mind mapping. I discussed a tool called Mindmap later in this book. This tool is simply to help you with the process; but even without the tool, you can get a piece of paper or a blank word document on your computer, a board, or an app on your devise; and do your brain dump.

Schedule time to spend for this process. You may want to dedicate 15 - 30 minutes to this.

Put down whatever comes to your mind. Don't try to analyze anything just yet, only put your thoughts down. If it will be easier for you to capture these ideas as a chart or some other form of drawings, don't hesitate to do so.

Whatever you choose, put your

ideas down. This will help you as you create your book outline later on.

Step 2: Create an Outline

Your outline is like a road map in your writing process. It helps you coordinate your thoughts in a logical order; and shows how to go from a starting point to a finished draft (your destination)

Some authors may write without a preset outline; but personally, I tend to be more productive with an outline, and definitely recommend using one.

There are no rigid rules for creating your book outline, but your brain dump can be a great asset here, as you create an outline from the ideas from your brain dump.

You can use index cards to create your outlines; or you may prefer note apps on your devices; or a word document. You may want to try different approaches to see what works best for you.

To create your outline, group the major ideas from your brain dump into different categories/sections, and summarize each section under one sentence that captures these ideas. These sections will serve as your individual chapters. You can always change this later on as you get more into your book writing, if you need to.

As you go through this process, add on any new ideas that come to mind on the topic you are writing about. Eliminate any ideas that don't work too well with your topic. You may also notice some repetitions during this process, remove such.

Always keep in mind what problem your book is solving, as this will be the focal point of all you write. Whatever your book title and blurb will promise is what you should aim to deliver in your writing.

Outlines are not carved in stones, so don't be afraid to move it around as you deem fit. The important thing is having something to guide you as you develop your book. The outline can be said to be a skeleton that you "flesh" out as you move from outline to your final draft.

Step 3: Develop the Chapters in Your Book

Organize the chapters identified from your outline and arrange them in an order that will enhance the flow of the message in your book.

Develop your sub-chapters. At this stage you want to write the key points that will be covered in each chapter. These are the important points you wish to highlight in that particular chapter.

Next step is to begin to develop the ideas to be covered in each chapter and sub-chapter.

Step 4: Write Your Book Introduction

Many good books have lost readers just because their introductions were poorly written. Needless to say, your book introduction plays a very crucial role in the success of your book.

Your introduction is your "sales copy" so to speak. In other words, it is like that sales write-up that you read and take action even before having time to rethink it. That is what you want your book introduction to do for you. It should be so inviting that the reader cannot wait to start reading your book!

Your introduction should pass on the message in your book, without giving away the full gist. It should leave the reader wanting more, and convinced they need your book, and need it NOW.

It is in this part of the book that you "sell" what you have to offer in the book. When I say "sell", I do not mean a dishonest promise, or a dishonest car sales man tactic; but rather a sincere and honest, yet strong promise of what your book will deliver.

In essence, your introduction should attract the reader, show them the benefit to be derived from reading your book (why they need your book); and there should be a call to action of some sort that culminates in them choosing, buying or downloading your book.

As you draft an introduction for your book, keep in mind the purpose of your book. If you are not completely sure of the entire purpose of your book yet, you can skip writing your introduction first, and write it after your draft is done, using what you have written as a guide. So, don't get stuck on the introduction if you're not absolutely sure yet all you will cover in your book.

In summary, your introduction should:

- Tell the reader what the book will do for them
- Show them why you qualify to show them what you know in the field you write about
- Be interesting enough to arouse

a reader's desire to read your book

- Help the reader chose to read your book

Step 5: Write the Body of Your Book

Using the chapters and sub-chapters created in step 3 above, write your first draft. Develop the ideas from your brain dump, as previously outlined, into meaningful sentences and paragraphs. Explain your ideas and points. Be as detailed and clear as possible.

To be most productive, try not to edit at this stage. Write as much and as fast as you possibly can. You will edit and fine-tune your writing later on in the process.

Step 6: Bring Your Book to a Close

(Conclusion):

If you wait for your book to be perfect before you round it up, then you never will. A very important aspect of your writing is bringing it to a conclusion.

As you write, chances are more chapters/sub-chapter ideas will keep coming to you, but you must know where to cut it off, so you can complete your book.

Be careful not to have too many varying topics in your book to avoid confusion. You cannot cover every topic that comes to your mind in this one book. Leave the other topics for your future books; otherwise you will never finish your book.

Chapter 7

Your Book Content

As you write your book, keep in mind that the following tips are crucial in this process.

Quality

First off, I must emphasize that quality cannot be negotiated. Give your very best into every book you write. Research if you need to, and interview experts if you must. Whatever you do, make it your best.

Your book should be good enough for any reader to feel excited about it enough to share it with someone else.

Sentences

Keep your sentences short and simple. Overly long sentences tend to become difficult to comprehend, and may lose their meaning.

Paragraphs

Use short to medium length paragraphs as much as possible. By all means avoid writing a whole page as one paragraph! It makes the book look really boring, and discourages the reader.

Imagine if this page you're reading is one long stretch of words; and the next pages look the same way. Before long, you will be bored. Make your paragraphs short and straight to the point. Avoid excessively long paragraphs as much as possible.

Make Your Points Clear

If you need to list certain points for better clarity, by all means do so. If you must use bullet points, do so as well. However, make sure your book is well balanced, and meaningful.

Use Simple Words

Beware of using unnecessary complicated words. Use simple, easy to understand words. No one wants to be checking the dictionary with every sentence they read in your book. This will put readers off.

Write in Conversational Tones

Your book should be like a good conversation - warm, inviting and interesting. As you finally begin to write, keep in mind that your writing can be likened to having a conversation. So see it as having a conversation with someone you are comfortable talking to.

Even if you don't like talking, you have thoughts, and most thoughts are conversational. Writing your book is simply putting your thoughts about a topic, or an issue down on paper. It's that simple!

Check Reviews on Books Similar to Yours

What I look for when I read such reviews are what the readers like most about the book. I also check the 1 star reviews to see why the readers were disappointed in the book. I also want to check if this a common opinion of majority of the readers that left the 1-2 star reviews.

If it is, then you need to take note of it. What this helps you do is to avoid making the same mistake that the readers are complaining about.

Sometimes it may be that the readers are expecting more than they got, or feel some vital points or parts were missing from the book. This is where you can help fill the void by providing (in addition to what you already have written) what is lacking in the other book that readers commonly complained about.

Remember you are targeting the same audience, and if you can give what they want, it puts you ahead of the game.

Length (How Long Should Your Book Be?)

You are writing a non-fiction that is aimed at answering questions, solving problems and meeting needs, therefore, it is best to not make it too long, if you don't have to. Make it short and straight to the point. Too much information can sometimes be overwhelming.

These days, people are looking for a quick read that offers solution, so keep it short, but not scanty. I had to warn against scantiness. As much as readers what straight-to-the-point books, it is annoying to buy a book, only for it to be no more than a pamphlet or brochure. Readers want some "meat" in what you are offering.

Also don't get stuck trying to write as many pages as possible. Many would-be authors never finish their books because they are trying to get it to 200 or more pages. This is good, but it is more important to give your message clearly than to fill up the book with irrelevant information.

Besides, if you do have so much information, you can always make a series out of your book topics, tackling a topic at a time in each book. This way, you more quickly finish your current book, and move on to the next.

Chapter 8

The Final Book Draft

Once your first draft is completed, it is time to take the next steps.

Read through your finished draft, correcting any spelling and grammatical errors you find. If possible have another set of eyes read your manuscript.

If you can afford it, consider engaging the services of a professional editor to help edit your book. Otherwise, re-read one more time checking for errors as you go. Don't be in too much of a hurry that you turn out a book full of errors!

You can hire freelance editors from

places like elance.com and odesk.com (now upwork.com)

If after editing, you are satisfied with the outcome, then congratulations! You have just completed writing your non-fiction book!

Chapter 9

Publishing Snapshots

An option available to you for getting published is to self-publish your book. Although this book is mainly to help you complete writing your non-fiction book, and have a manuscript ready to publish, I will be giving you some snapshots to publishing your book on Amazon in this chapter.

Publishing on Amazon

Once you are ready to publish your book, Amazon is a great way to get your book in front of millions of readers, especially if you are just starting out as an Author.

Your completed draft can be published on Amazon's Kindle Direct Publishing (KDP) as an eBook in as little as a few hours. What you need is your formatted manuscript, and a book cover. To get more information on this, visit https://kdp.amazon.com/

Why Amazon?

There are several other platforms nowadays where you can self-publish your book. However, I have chosen to concentrate on Amazon because of the many advantages it offers you as an Author. Some of which are listed below:

- **Huge Audience/Market Share:** These days, more and more people are turning online for their purchases, particularly when it comes to buying books. Amazon already has an established market that attracts millions of readers worldwide, so Amazon is a wonderful option when it comes to selling books.

- **Minimal Cost:** When you publish with Amazon, you incur very little cost. In fact your costs will basically be related to other factors needed to get your book ready to publish such as book cover, or formatting costs, if you choose to outsource those. The actual process of publishing on Amazon is free. You are not charged to get your book published.

- **You Keep the Bulk of Your Profits:** When you publish with Amazon kindle, you get to keep as much as 70% of the revenue generated from your book!

- **Print-On-Demand:** For your print books (paperbacks) published through CreateSpace, you don't have to pay to print hundreds of your book at once, if you don't need that many.

  Since your books are printed to order, you only order and pay for the quantities you need. This is a great way to control your costs. Amazon also help sell your books by printing and shipping to customers as orders are made on Amazon.

- **Free Amazon Advertisement:** Amazon markets your book by listing them in search results as customers search for books similar to yours. Your books could also be featured as part of the books being bought by customers searching for a particular book. In addition, Amazon sends emails to their list promoting books sold on Amazon.

What You Need to be Published

The Book Cover

Yes, readers do judge the book by the cover: You probably have heard it said times without number "don't judge the book by the cover"; but when it comes to books, readers do judge the book by its cover! If you will be putting up your book on online platforms like Amazon, where there are lots of competitions, it is very important to have a really good book cover.

Your book cover must be attractive: It must be attractive enough to draw a potential reader to click on it for more information.

Fonts Matter: It is also very important that the fonts on the cover are bold and legible enough for anyone browsing through the listed books to be able to quickly read your book title. People want information fast, and many don't have the patience to first click on a book before knowing what it's about.

Relevance: Your book cover must be relevant to your topic. You cannot, for example have a cookbook, and use the photo of a flashy car on your book cover; that just won't make sense to someone looking for a cookbook. If anything at all, it will be very confusing.

Keep it Simple: It is important to keep things as simple as possible. Avoid overcrowding your book cover with photos, fonts, etc. As much as you can, maintain a simple, easy to read book cover and title.

You can create your covers yourself using Amazon templates. However, except you are good at graphic designs and know what you are doing, I will suggest you use a professional for your covers.

These days you can get professional looking covers at reasonable costs from freelancers online.

Book Formatting

Not having your book formatted properly can cause readers to leave you negative reviews! So pay attention to getting your book well formatted. This is even more important for eBooks. If it means getting professional help, by all means do so. Otherwise, you can also take advantage of several book formatting software such as Kinstant, for example.

Scrivener is also a great tool you can use to export your manuscript as an eBook (.mobi or .pub). See the section on Scrivener in Chapter 7 for more on this tool.

Getting your book ready for print is pretty easy. CreateSpace provides you with downloadable templates you can use to upload your work. These templates come in different sizes depending on what your choice is. You can find these templates at https://www.createspace.com/en/com munity/docs/DOC-1323

Places to get help for your book

Formatting, Book Covers, Editing and the likes can be outsourced to professionals. Here are some sites where you can get professionals to help with these aspects of your book.

Odesk.com (now upwork.com)

Fiverr.com

Guru.com

Elance.com

What Attracts Readers to Your Book

Writing a good book is excellent, but there are other factors necessary to get your book picked up by a reader.

As you are well aware, there are millions of books out there on Amazon, for instance; and one of the things that will help sell your book are reviews.

However reviews are not only based on the quality of the book; there are many other factors that can cause a well written, good book to get negative reviews, and so discourage other readers from picking it up to buy and read. It is important to consider these other factors, and use them to your advantage.

To attract readers and put your book in a better position for positive reviews/feedbacks, pay attention to the following:

Pricing Your Book:

Set a fair competitive price for your book. A good rule of thumb is to research what similar books as yours are being sold for. If you are a brand new author that is not yet known, you may want to price your book a little lower than other books in your genre. You can raise the price later as you begin to build loyal readers.

Reviews:

Reviews can build or break a book! Get your book reviewed as soon as possible after your launch date.

You can also try getting reviews even before your book is launched by sharing your manuscripts with people willing to read and review before your launch date.

Positive reviews lend credibility to your book, which is another reason you need to work at having quality content in your book. Don't just write for writing sake or just to brag you are an author.

Write with purpose; purpose to help someone else through the information you are providing in your book.

Referrals/Word of Mouth:

You may have people specifically searching out your titles because someone spoke highly of your book to them. This, of course, is also some form of reviews. Even though more informal in nature, it works just as great in getting loyal fans and book sales.

Chapter 10

Your Author Productivity Tools

A tool is simply something that aides in the performance of a task. Every profession has its own tools, helping to make the job easier and flow more smoothly. Writing is no exception.

There are many tools available to you as an Author that will help you write your book much faster and with fewer difficulties.

While many of these tools will make your job as an Author much easier, it is not mandatory that you have them all to be able to write a good book, or to be a bestselling Author. But they are worth mentioning, so you know what is available.

When I first started writing I knew very little, if anything, about most of these tools. But as I wrote, studied, and researched more, I became aware of these different tools, and consequently became more efficient in my writing.

Again, you don't need to have all of these to be able to write a book, so don't let that be a reason to procrastinate. You should go with what you feel most comfortable with, what works best for you as an individual, that is.

If you are more comfortable doing your writing using pen and paper, by all means use those, and get it typed out later.

The important thing is to use the methods that work best for you. There is however no harm in knowing what these tools are, and how to use them if possible.

Personally, I make use of any tool that can help me write better and faster. Be open to explore writing tools you come across, and pick the ones that help you to be most productive.

Below are some of the tools available to you as an Author:

MindMap

There are software and applications that will help you do your brain dump, as you think about the ideas you will be sharing in your book. They come in different names. Examples of these are "FreeMind", and TheBrain for personal computers; and "SimpleMind" for mobile devices.

You will find several more by searching online (or the app store) for "mindmap". Check the reviews on them, to decide which one you prefer.

Scrivener

This is a powerful tool that is increasingly becoming more and more popular among writers. It helps you organize and generate your book content with much greater ease. It is designed specifically for writers, in that it has so many capabilities that enhance your writing.

Scrivener will even help you plan your writing. You can set a deadline, and it will calculate how many words you need to write daily, for example. Another great feature is the ability to directly export your book into eBook formats (pub and mobi). This saves you the money you would have spent to get someone else do your formats.

You can get a free trial at http://www.authorselfpublishtips.com/recommended-tools-products/

Computers

This is a must have, even if you are one that prefer to do your first draft with pen and paper. You will need your computer (either laptop or desktop) for more than just writing your book. In fact without a computer, you may not be able to access many of the other tools, because you need to download these software onto your computer.

For your writing, formatting, emailing/communication etc, you will need a personal computer, so do invest in a good one. Fortunately there are cheap effective computers around these days.

To write your book on your computer, you will need at least a word processor. Having a Microsoft Word document installed on your computer is sufficient to write and complete your book.

Even if you use no other tool, make sure you are comfortable to a degree using Microsoft Word document (or similar document). Spend time to learn the basics, at least - typing, simple formatting etc. If you need help with this, you can find some good tutorials on YouTube.

You will also need internet access, especially for you to be able to download your book on to the publishing platforms you choose.

Mobile Devices (iPad/Tablets)

IPads and tablets can be very comfortable, light-weighted companions on your writing journey. With so many note apps to choose from, it has never been easier to do your writing on your devices.

If you have a very busy life, or find it hard to carry a laptop everywhere you go, this is an excellent alternative. Although you still need to transfer (sync) your work to your computer, but at least you can continue with your book, even when you don't have your laptop with you.

Most tablets will fit into a lady's purse, even with the Bluetooth keyboards on! I used an iPad a lot as I wrote some of my books on the train and public buses. I found it really convenient, and would sync to my computer once I got a chance. It helped me get a lot of writing done, even in places that wouldn't have been too comfortable for a laptop.

If you decide to use an iPad or a tablet for writing, choose apps that you can easily sync with your computer; that way you will save a lot of time. Examples of such app that I have used for so many years is the "docs to go" app. I am not endorsing this app, but simply sharing what has worked for me in the past.

If you'll like a list of recommended products, tools, and trainings, please visit http://www.authorselfpublishtips.com/ recommended-tools-products/

RALI MACAULAY

30 Day Writing Plan

Because our time availability and life activities differ, this plan is a suggestion to get you to at least finish your book, and be ready for the next stages of editing, formatting, publishing etc. Feel free to tweak as much as you need to.

Writing a book is doable in 30 days or less, but know that it requires some work and discipline from you. There have been good quality books written in this time frame or even sooner. Until you plan, start and stick to your plan, you'll never know what you are capable of accomplishing.

This plan is to help you keep going. If you slack behind, don't give up. Restructure, and continue writing. Keep your end result in mind and you will succeed!

As explained in an earlier chapter, your book does not need to be any particular number of pages. Shorter books will, of course, take you lesser time to complete. But even longer ones can be written in a month. So be encouraged.

Day 1:

- Create the right environment to do your writing (designate your writing spot)

- Using the methods described in chapter 4 "Choosing a Book Topic", decide on what topic/idea you are writing on.

Day 2:

- Do a brain dump.

- Draft your book outline. Make it as detailed as you can. Move around and tweak as needed.

- Decide on number of chapters, and/or the total word count for your book.

Days 3 through 24:

- Start writing your first draft. Devote as much time as you can to it. Leave editing for later, just write as much and as fast as you can. If it helps better, divide the number of chapters (or words) you have decided on based on the number of days you have to do your first draft, and maximize your time. During this time, start working on your cover as well. The earlier you get a cover done, the better.

If you were able to complete these tasks, in the time allotted, congratulations. If not, don't fret; use the remaining days from your 30 days to keep writing your manuscript.

But if you are done writing, then it's time for to proceed to the next stage.

Next Steps

Now that your first draft is completed, congratulations! It is time for next steps. The publishing process is beyond the scope of this particular book, but below is a brief explanation of what your next steps will be.

Days 25 through 27:

- Edit, edit, and edit again. Thoroughly edit your first draft to the best of your ability. The edited work will be your second draft.

Days 28 through 29:

- Reread your second draft. It is strongly advisable to read it out loud to test how it sounds in your ears. If you have a trusted friend or family member, you may want to have them read it too, if they're available. Make any additional corrections as needed. You now have your final draft! You did it! Now you are ready to publish your book.

Day 30:

- Publish on Amazon.

Congratulations!!! You are now an Author!

RALI MACAULAY